JOURNEY TO THE PAST

CLASSICAL ATHENS

Mario Denti

A Harcourt Company

Austin • New York
www.steck-vaughn.com

Copyright © 2001, text, Steck-Vaughn Company

Copyright © 1998 Istituto Geografico De Agostini, Novara

All rights reserved. No part of this book may be reproduced or utilized in any form or by any means, electronic or mechanical, including photocopying, recording, or by any information storage and retrieval system, without permission in writing from the Publisher. Inquiries should be addressed to: Copyright Permissions, Steck-Vaughn Company, P.O. Box 26015, Austin, TX 78755

Published by Raintree Steck-Vaughn, an imprint of Steck-Vaughn Company

Library of Congress Cataloging-in-Publication Data

Denti, Mario.
   Classical Athens / Marco Denti.
     p. cm. — (Journey to the past)
   Includes index.
   ISBN 0-7398-1953-4
    1. Athens (Greece)—Civilization—Juvenile literature. 2. Greece—Civilization—to 146 B.C.—Juvenile literature. [1. Athens (Greece)—Civilization. 2. Greece—Civilization—to 146 B.C.] I. Title. II. Series.

DF275 .D36 2001
938'.5—dc21   00-059201

Translated by: Mary Stuttard
Editorial Director: Cristina Cappa Legora
Editor: Stefano Sibella
Illustrations: Aldo Ripamonti
Graphics: Marco Volpati

Raintree Steck-Vaughn Staff: Marion Bracken, Pam Wells
Project Manager: Lyda Guz
Photo Research: Claudette Landry, Sarah Fraser

Photo Credits:

P.48a ©Superstock; p.48b ©Tom Trill/Stone; p.49a ©John Callahan/Stone; p.49b ©CORBIS; p.50a ©CORBIS; p. 51a ©John Mason/The Stock Market

All other photographs are from the Archives of IGDA.

Printed and bound in Italy

1 2 3 4 5 6 7 8 9 05 04 03 02 01 00

Table of Contents

Guidebook 4
  All Roads Lead to Athens! 4
  Welcome! 6
The Upper Town 12
  The Acropolis 12
  The Parthenon 14
  The Festivals of Athena 16
The Lower Town 18
  The Agora 18
  The Council 20
Education and Health 22
  The High School and Gymnasium 22
  The Asclepieion 24
Entertainment 26
  The Theater 26
  The Stadium 28
Arts and Crafts 30
  The Potter's Workshop 30
  The Workshop Where Bronzes Are Made 32
Houses and Customs 34
  The Home 34
  The Symposium 36
Trips Outside the City 38
  The Necropolis of Dipylon 38
  The Sanctuary of Delphi 40
  Attica: The Territory Surrounding Athens 42
  The Port of Piraeus 45
The Armed Forces 46
  Athens: War 46
Athens Today 48
Some Important Facts 52
Glossary 53
Further Reading 54
Index 55–56

Guidebook

All Roads Lead to Athens!

If you have the time and you enjoy wandering through a country in order to discover it, you can venture along the roads that cross Greece until, tired and worn by the hazards you will certainly meet during your journey, you arrive in Athens. But if you are in a hurry to admire the many treasures the city has in store for you, set sail on the first ship heading for Piraeus.

People usually travel on foot along the few, impassable roads that cross Attica. They travel alone or in the company of a slave, struggling under the weight of their luggage. It is tiring to travel along such rough, risky roads. You can travel by mule cart over long distances or across relatively flat regions. The roads are not lit, and it is

advisable to travel during daylight hours and reach your destination before sunset. Most Greeks find traveling by sea a better alternative, although the ever-present, blustery wind that blows across the Aegean Sea can make sailing difficult. Besides the small cargo vessels do not always appear very safe.

By sea your journey will be quicker if you follow the regular trade routes. If you sail to Athens from the East, that is, the Orient, you will dock at the wharves in Piraeus, the port for the Greek capital. If you arrive from the West, Athens is visible from the Gulf of Corinth. You can avoid sailing around the Peloponnese by crossing the thin strip of land that separates the Peloponnese from the region of Saronikos thanks to an ingenious device. There is a special canal bordered by a road paved in stone which has channels, or grooves, to allow specially-designed carts to pull the ships and their crews as far as the sea!

Heroes and Navigators

The lack of land for farming, almost exclusively owned by a small number of aristocrats, has been responsible for the high level of emigration from Greece since ancient times. People sailed away to seek their fortunes in new countries around the Mediterranean. On the map you can see where the colonists settled: to the east, along the coasts of Asia Minor and the Black Sea; to the west, principally in southern Italy, where they founded the flourishing civilizations of Magna Grecia and where later splendid cities rose at the center of fertile agricultural regions. Despite the intense trade exchanges, the new territories are governed locally and are politically independent from the homeland that their inhabitants came from.

Acragas/Agrigento; Apollonia; Aspendus; Athenae/Athens; Byzantium/Istanbul; Caulonia; Celenderis; Chius/Kòs/Santorini; Corcyra/Corfu; Corinthus/Corinth; Creta/Crete; Croton/Crotone; Cyprus/Cyprus; Cyrene/Cyrene; Cumae/Cuma; Elea/Velia; Emporion; Ephesus/Ephesus; Epidaurus/Epidaurus; Epidamnus/Druazzo/Durrës; Gela/Gela; Lesbus/Lesbos; Locri; Massalia/Marseilles; Megara Hyblaea; Metapontum/Metaponto; Miletus/Mileto; Naxos; Neapolis/Naples; Odessus/Odessa; Pergamum/Pergamo; Pontus Euxinus/Black Sea; Poseidonia/ Paestum; Reghion/Reggio Calabria; Rhodus/Rhodes; Samus/Samos; Selinus/Selinunte; Sesamus; Sinope/Sinop; Siris; Sparta/Sparta; Sybaris/Sibari; Syracusae/Syracuse; Tarentum/Taranto; Tomis/Costanza; Trapezus/Trebisonda. The names that have not been transcribed are archaeological sites, no longer active cities or commercial centers.

Guidebook

Welcome!

As you approach Athens, the Acropolis, the sacred hill that dominates the city, will suddenly appear before you. It is a striking vision in white, hard and solid as marble, gleaming like the reflection of a wave on the sea. Over time the city has grown and developed at its feet. Most likely you will have reached Athens by the road that connects it to Eleusis. This is the sacred way for all Greeks. Near the city you will come across the necropolis, or burial area, called Dipylon. This is the area used for burying the dead. Continue in the same direction, and soon you will find yourself in a part of the city named the Ceramico. This is one of the most thickly populated and bustling parts of Athens. Its network of narrow, winding

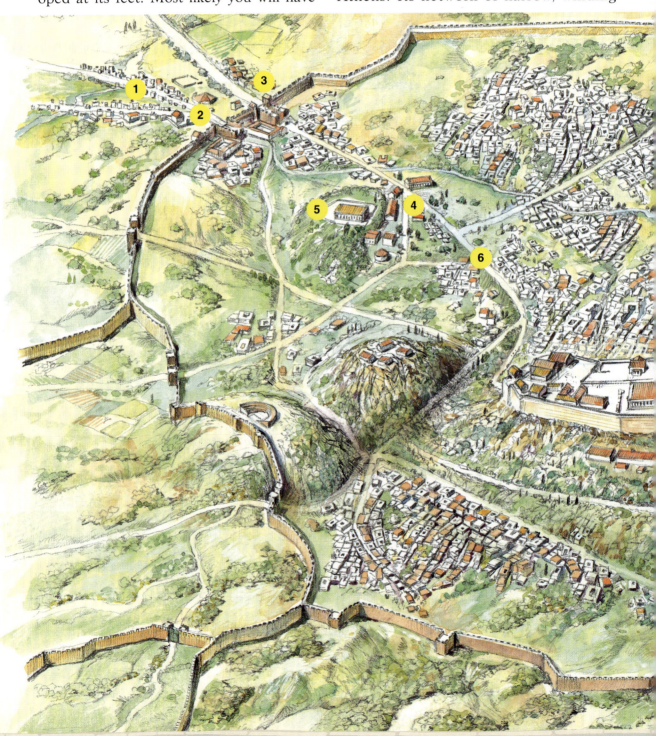

streets are crowded with poor houses belonging to the local craftsmen, tiny shops, and potters' workshops. Once you have entered the fortified walls surrounding the city, which are equal to the length of about 30 stadiums, Athens will spread out before you. The building developments have spread especially out to the west, around the hills, the Acropolis, the Colonus, the Agoraios, the Hill of the Nymphs, the Pnice, the Mouseion, the Licabethus, and the Ardettus. Inside the city walls, you will still find vast areas of land that have not yet been built on or that have been cultivated as vegetable gardens. A little farther along the Sacred Way you will come into Panatenee Street. Go along it and you will pass through the Agora—the huge market square. Keep going—the rest of the city is just waiting to be discovered.

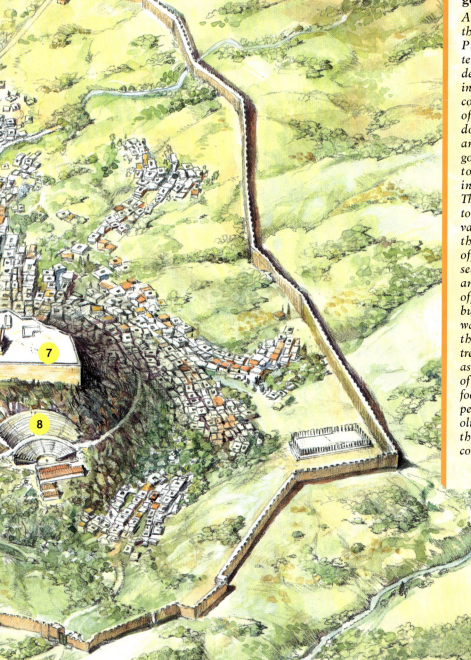

How did Athens get its name?

Athens was named after the goddess Athena. The Parthenon, the largest temple on the Acropolis, is dedicated to her. According to the legend, in the contest over the possession of Attica, between Poseidon, the god of the sea, and Athena, the warrior goddess triumphed, thanks to the judgment of the inhabitants of the city. They decided that her gift to the city was of greater value and more useful to their future than that offered by the god of the sea. Athena offered them an olive plant. Poseidon offered a spring of water, but one from which salty water flowed. Since then the olive tree has been treasured as a sacred tree as well as being the basis of the local economy and food supply. What is more, people say the color of the olive tree's leaves reminds them of the gray-green color of Athena's eyes.

1. Sacred Way
2. Dipylon
3. Potters' Quarter
4. Agora
5. Pnice
6. Panatenee Street
7. Acropolis
8. Theater of Dionysus

GUIDEBOOK

Useful Information

Once inside Athens, do not imagine you will find yourself faced with a vast, impressive metropolis full of services, public works, elegant restaurants, and meeting places. Instead you will be struck by the strong contrast between the public and private sides of the city. First, there are the areas used for religious practices, the temples on the Acropolis, or the political and public activities, the Agora, with its public buildings like the theater, the stadium, and the gymnasium. Then, there are the residential areas where the majority of Athenians live and work. The temples and public buildings are extremely well cared for by the State and by private citizens who compete to make them even more beautiful and worthy of attention. By contrast, side by side with this "official" face of Athens there is another poorer, humbler side of the city where the people live out their lives.

Most Athenians live in very modest if not crumbling houses without any modern conveniences like toilets or running water. They are crowded together and have developed mostly toward the northwest. They have been constructed with the cheapest building materials: wood, skins, straw mats, and bricks crudely made from a mixture of mud and water dried in the sun. These materials are very different from the precious marble used on the Acropolis.

Almost all the houses, even the better quality ones, face onto alleys and narrow, winding streets. They are built clinging to hills, which become rushing torrents when it rains. The neighborhoods are considered to be quite risky, especially at night, when the chance of unpleasant encounters greatly increases.

MONEY

The most widespread coin in Greece is the drachma, which in the region of Attica weighs about 4.36 grams of silver. There is also the mina worth 100 drachmas and the talent, worth 60 minas or 6,000 drachmas. For small change the Athenians use the obolo, equal to about one sixth of a drachma.

The Athenian coins, found throughout the Mediterranean, are easily recognized. On one face is the crowned head of Athena and on the other the image of an owl and an olive branch, the bird and plant sacred to the goddess. Look carefully and you will see the inscription ATHE, the initials of the name of the city.

Each Greek city-state mints its own coins and each has its own value, thus making conversion, or changing, from one type of money to another very difficult. So if you are asked to pay 10 obolos at the market for the best fish, you really need to know if they mean Attican obolos or those from Egina, worth 3/10ths more. A lyre or oboe player earns 2 drachmas a day, and a laborer only 1. That is far too little to live on, however modestly.

WHERE TO EAT AND SLEEP?

Inns, hostels, and restaurants are of an extremely low level in the ancient Greek world! It is better to stay with a friend, preferably someone who is well-to-do. If lunch appears rather frugal, in the evening you will be able to enjoy the delights of a symposium, a banquet reserved for people of the higher social classes. You will also be able to rest on something like a real bed.

If you don't have a prosperous friend, you will have to make do with staying in a private home, where for a small fee you can find refuge for the night and something simple to eat. In summer the coolest place to sleep is the terrace of the house. From there on a clear night, you will be able to enjoy the splendor of a starry Greek night and be lulled to sleep by a chorus of crickets.

Addresses, Curiosities, Gestures

In the winding labyrinth of Athenian streets and alleys, it is almost impossible to find any points of reference to help you recognize places. The city has no organized network of roads, and the narrow streets in the residential areas are little more than passageways between the houses.

The Athenians have a colorful and expressive way of speaking. Understanding their body language and gestures may prove extremely useful if you need to ask for information. For example, to say "no" the Greeks do not shake their heads—a head movement which, on the contrary, means "yes"—but they tip their heads backwards.

To show happiness they raise a hand while snapping their fingers. To mock someone they show a fist and point their middle finger. Spitting on the floor is more widespread than you might imagine and is a form of superstition. It is used to cancel the effect of an unfavorable word, meeting, or ominous warning. The Greeks do not shake hands to greet each other, but only in solemn moments or during ritual celebrations.

Clothing

For strolling around Athens, it is really practical and comfortable to wear the clothes worn by the locals. There is really only one model for the traveler. This is a simple, rectangular piece of material wound around the body in different styles, but there are not many variations. The ordinary people, the workers and laborers, wear a simple, short tunic. It is held at the waist by a buckle, or by a knot that leaves one shoulder free and one part of the body bare.

The chiton is the most popular garment. It is used by both men and women. The chiton is a light, linen tunic of varying lengths and fixed by a buckle on both shoulders. Over their chiton the Greeks often wear a long, woolen cloak which keeps them warm and protects them from bad weather. Young men and armed men, such as soldiers and horsemen, wear a short cloak. Many Athenian women enjoy wearing a shawl over their chiton. This is especially popular with Spartan women.

Except for slaves and the poor, the Athenians wear sandals or boots in different styles. At home they enjoy going barefoot. No one wears a hat! Only travelers, foreigners, and strangers to the city wear a wide-brimmed hat made from felt or straw to protect them from the burning sun.

What to do if you are sick

Should you get sick during your stay in Athens, rest assured that the city is well-served by pharmacies where you can find useful forms of medication made from herbs and medicinal plants. It is the doctors themselves who know the formulas and ingredients of these natural treatments and who make up the preparations. If you need an appointment, they will receive you directly in their homes. Athens has a public health service managed by the State. The doctors who work for the public are chosen by the citizens' assembly and are paid by the community with the proceeds from a special tax for this purpose. There are specialists too! The dentists are famous for treating patients' teeth with lead fillings and the oculists for their effective use of eye washes.

It is important to remember that the art of medicine has a long and well-established history in Greece. This tradition is linked to the important schools of medicine which have developed in different centers throughout the Mediterranean, such as Cnido, Crotone, and above all Kos. This is the island where Hippocrates was born. He is famous for being the founder of medicine as a separate science, based on experience, direct practice, and reason. This science aimed to relieve the patient's suffering also by using the stimulus of the natural healing powers in the body. Hippocratic medicine has developed alongside the other remedies widespread in Greece. At times these are confused with magic or the interpretation of dreams practiced in the Asclepieion temple. Apart from learning the techniques of the prevention and cure of illnesses, the pupils of Hippocrates also learn to observe a moral code, the Hippocratic Oath, in which the doctors recognize the sacred side of their art and pledge to respect the patient's medical secret and vow never to harm their patients in any way.

Guidebook

What can you eat in Athens?

Athenians eat three or four times a day. In the morning they eat a breakfast of barley or wheat bread, soaked in a little wine, sometimes accompanied by figs or olives. At midday they eat a frugal meal, then they stop for a mid-afternoon snack. At sunset, dinner, the evening meal, is eaten. Though not a sumptuous meal it is a little more varied and abundant than lunch. The menu is mainly vegetarian and completes the rather frugal diet of the lower Athenian classes.

The basic ingredients of Greek cuisine, always present at table, are barley and wheat. With water and barley flour they make special biscuits, which replace the more popular wheat bread eaten on special holidays. Greens are not cheap. The Athenians prefer onions and olives, broad beans and lentils, from which they make excellent soups and purees. Cheese is quite plentiful, but meat is rare, except for pork. Seafood is very popular, especially octopus and squid caught along the coasts of Euboea, one of Greece's largest islands. Favorite desserts are walnuts, grapes, honey cakes, dried figs, and fresh fruit.

You will have to get used to eating with your hands, since there is no cutlery. Knives are only used for cutting meat or cheese and spoons for soup and purees. Food is served on plates or in bowls made from terracotta covered with a shiny, black varnish, which looks like metal. You will only see bronze and silver vases on the tables of the rich.

Wine is sipped at dinner, but Athens also has excellent water, to which people sometimes add honey. The Athenians find goat's milk refreshing too, as well as a thick drink made from barley flour, water, and flavored with mint or thyme. You might enjoy tasting it when you have eaten too much garlic!

Where to go Shopping

It is not easy to find the shops in the confusion of Athen's narrow, winding streets. You will just have to get used to it! Be alert, glance into courtyards, and do not be afraid to ask a passerby.

To have some idea of what is on sale, you can begin by visiting the Agora and its surrounding streets, which lead up to the foot of the Acropolis. Here, especially during the lively Dionysian festivals, at the end of March, merchants and craftsmen gather for a huge market, which attracts many foreigners to Athens. You can find everything: leather, materials, objects in wood, terracotta or ceramics, basic foodstuffs, meat, fish, cheese, game, fruit, and vegetables.

Should problems arise about prices or if you feel the goods are not being weighed correctly, you can ask for the help of a state civil servant whose job is to check the fair value of the products and to make sure the market runs smoothly and to see there are no robberies or disorders of any kind. The evaluation of weights and measures is trusted to special inspectors.

Weights and Measures

Different systems of measurement exist in the Greek world depending on the need. For liquids the smallest unit is equal to 1.5 ounces. The largest is around 15 gallons. This may be divided into 12 even smaller units. The 15-gallon size is equal to the average content of an amphora, a two-handled, terracotta container used for the commercial transportation of olive oil, wine, and beverages. To measure out cereals, wheat, flour and vegetables, the Greeks use several sizes, such as the .5 pint size, and the 1.5 bushel-size. For weighing they use a 1.75 quart weight.

Each year 400,000 of the 1.5 bushel size of wheat are sent from the major suppliers around the Euxine Sea (the Black Sea) to supply Athens. This amounts to over 600,000 bushels! To measure length, the basic unit is equal to around 12.5 inches. To calculate distance, the Greeks normally use the *stadio,* equal to about 590 feet.

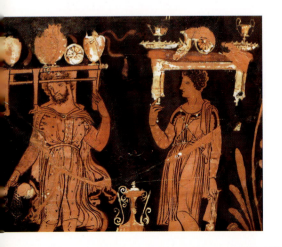

Hours and the Calendar

The Greeks find it easy to measure time as they have invented two instruments that work precisely, the gnomon, a kind of sundial, and the water clock. The day begins for everyone at sunrise and ends when darkness falls.

The Athenian calendar is fixed according to the religious festivals and holidays. The year officially begins in July, when the end of the harvest and the god of the crops are celebrated in the Kronia. At the end of the month comes the solemn festival of Panatenee. This is followed by the months of August, September, and October.

October is the time of year when the people make offerings of vegetables and broadbeans to the god Apollo, and an olive branch bound in strips of wool and decorated with early fruit and vegetables is displayed in processions to ask the gods for fertility. After the festival of Thesmoforie, in honor of Demeter, the month closes with the celebrations dedicated to the gods of the blacksmiths and the craftsmen. The worship of Poseidon in December begins the cycle of Dionysian festivals, which finish at the end of winter in March.

Children in Athens

At home or in the city streets the Athenian children play with balls, hoops, dice, swings, yo-yos, and with various types of toys made from wood or terracotta, for example, carts, small horses, tops, dolls with jointed limbs. They might invite you to play marbles with them, using walnuts. Another game they enjoy is where you have to hit a target with a stone or a ball. The winner can ask the loser for a piggyback ride to anywhere they choose. Another popular game is where you have to show your skill at throwing stones or pieces of a broken pot as near as possible to a line drawn on the ground.

The important public or religious festivals are often occasions for enjoyment too. For example, during the festival of "Antesterie," at the end of February, you can buy wonderful toys made by craftsmen or watch performances by mimes, clowns, magicians, jugglers, and dancers.

The Athenian children spend a long time outdoors in the company of their domestic animals, such as dogs, cats, hens, and perhaps the old family mule.

The Athenians, what curious people!

Few Athenians can afford not to take the title of Greek citizen seriously. A citizen has the right to be a member of the *demos*, the people, and thus enjoys political rights, plus the right to take part in the state assembly, where all the important decisions concerning the life of the *polis*, or city-state, are taken.

Each citizen has three names: their first name, their father's name, and the *deme*, or local government they belong to. For example: Pericles, son of Santippe, from the deme of Colarges. The right to citizenship is determined by two factors. First you must be 18 years old (which in practice becomes 20 years old) when you have finished your education and have served your military service. Secondly, both your father and mother must be Athenian.

Taking an active part in the governing of your *polis* demands a lot of time and a certain economic ease, because the administrative jobs do not go well with a professional activity. Thus the political freedom of just a few people is based on the efforts made and the jobs performed by other categories of people, especially slaves and metics, or foreigners who live in the city. Even though foreigners have to pay taxes and serve in the army, they have no political rights. They work as craftsmen or merchants, principally in the sectors of cloth-making, leather and skins, pottery, and metalwork. They sometimes become quite wealthy.

Slaves, on the other hand, are excluded from life in society, despite the fact that as a workforce they are the major economic drivers of the city. They are considered no more than beasts of burden. The cities in Attica buy their slaves at the market, like goods, or they deport groups of peoples they have defeated in war to become slaves in Greece. Finally, what can we say about the plight of Greek women, who have no civil rights and are forced to live out their lives closed inside their homes.

THE UPPER TOWN

The Acropolis

Once in Athens go immediately to visit the Acropolis, the highest part of the city. Originally, a small group of houses belonging to farmers and shepherds who worshiped owls and serpents surrounded the king's palace here. Over time the Acropolis has changed from being a fortified stronghold and the political and administrative heart of the city to the seat of many sacred buildings and the center of the cult of Athena, the goddess who Athenians believe protects their city.

To climb up the Acropolis, take the sacred way of the Panatenee (1) until you reach the impressive entrance to the sanctuary (2), from there you will be able to enjoy a magnificent view of Athens and its surrounding area. On clear days you can see as far as the port of Piraeus and the open sea. The horizon seems to blend with the blue Attican sky.

As you enter the sanctuary, look to the right and you will see the small ionic temple (3) dedicated to Athena Nike, or Athena Victorious. Once over the threshold of the monuments, you will find the sanctuary of Artemis Brauronia (4), the bear-god, who is venerated with special celebrations every four years, in springtime. Young girls are disguised as bears and wear saffron-colored robes for these festivities. Next you will see the place (5) where rows of engraved bronze offerings are kept. Right in front of you, towers the Parthenon (6), the most important temple on the Acropolis. Behind the Parthenon rises the *temenos* of Zeus Polieus (7) and the altar of Athena (8).

Alongside the Parthenon you will see a small temple (9) called the Erechtheion. It is dedicated to the worship of Poseidon and Athena. Nearby is the statue of Athena Promachos (10).

How beautiful the Acropolis is!

We owe the beauty and splendor of the Acropolis to the initiative of Pericles, in the 5th century B.C. After the destruction suffered during the Persian Wars, the splendid marble, the harmony of the architectural forms, and the wealth of the sculptured decorations were chosen to celebrate the renewed political power of the Athenian democracy, together with its ruling influence in the Mediterranean. For this huge task Pericles engaged the talents of the best architects—Callicrates, Ictinus, and Mnesicles—and the best sculptor, Phidias.

A crowded sanctuary

In the sanctuary on the Acropolis many votive statues are to be found. They were erected to commemorate an important event, a military victory, a danger escaped or in honor of one of the gods worshiped by the Athenians. Some of the most important are the Trojan Horse, the group of Athena and Marsia, the statue of Athena Lemnia, gift of the colonists on the island of Lemnos, and the gigantic statue of Athena Promachos by Phidias. This statue is 30 feet high, and, since it can be seen from far away, it bids sailors and travelers welcome as they approach the city.

The Upper Town

The Parthenon

After wandering around the magnificent buildings on the Acropolis, stop to admire the Parthenon, which the Athenians like to call "the big temple." You will be amazed by the grandeur of its white marble columns. This white marble was hewn from the nearby Mount Pentelico and reflects the light in a most impressive way. Look carefully at the wonderful decorations sculptured on the fronton, or pediment, and on the marble relief on the upper part of the temple which tell the ancient stories of the gods and the myths of Greece.

On the western pediment, Athena and Poseidon compete for the control of Attica. Along the sides of the building, the rectangular spaces in the friezes are decorated with bas-relief figures of Giants, Titans, Centaurs, and Amazons created to celebrate the victory of the Greek civilization over the Persians, who were considered barbaric and backward.

On the eastern pediment, over the entrance to the temple, which always faces the east in sacred buildings to greet the rising sun, you can see a scene of the gods watching the birth of Athena from the head of Zeus. Once inside the temple, after the entrance porch, you will find yourself in the chapel, the most sacred part of the temple, where the god or goddess is believed to be present. Look up and you will see a wonderful frieze that shows the Panatenee procession running all the way around the walls.

Right in front of you, rises the huge statue of Athena Parthenos, the Virgin Athena, goddess and protectress of the city. Erect and solemn, dressed in a long chiton, armed with a shield and lance, a shield on her breast, a goatskin with the frightful head of the Gorgon Medusa surrounded by snakes, the goddess holds the figure of Athena Nike on her hand.

Precious treasures

The Parthenon took only 16 years to build. The architects were Ictinus and Callicrates. The temple houses the monumental statue of Athena by the sculptor Phidias, who was the superintendent of the arts responsible for the artistic work in the temple. The statue is 40 feet high, stands on a huge decorated base and is made from ivory and gold. The cloak alone weighs a ton! There is a pool of water in the chapel to help keep the atmosphere humid in order to preserve the ivory. On the completion of this precious masterpiece, Phidias was accused of having sold some of the valuable materials to make a personal profit.

Her helmet is decorated with a sphinx and two winged horses, and at her feet the snake of Heritonius rests on a vast decorated base.

Harmony and balance

All of Athens contributed to the building of the Parthenon, working side by side with the famous artists. There were carpenters, sculptors, foundrymen, stonecutters, gilders, painters, decorators, chiselers, laborers, and those who transported materials by land and sea. Then there were merchants, sailors, carters, drivers, rope-makers, weavers, saddlers, bakers, shopkeepers, cooks, and shepherds, together with a large number of donkeys, mules, and horses. The total cost of the Parthenon alone was 700 talents, over 4 million drachmas!

THE UPPER TOWN

The Festivals of Athena

On the 28th of July, the birthday of the goddess Athena, do not miss the opportunity of taking part in the Panathenaea, the elaborate festivals celebrated every four years in her honor. After a long night's vigil, a solemn procession sets off from the potters' quarter. It winds along the Sacred Way, crosses the Agora, to finally arrive at the Acropolis. Here over a hundred sheep and oxen are sacrificed on the altar dedicated to the goddess, then their meat is distributed to the people.

The procession is headed by young maidens who are devoted to the cult of Athena. They live in the Parthenon, in the virgins' chambers just behind the temple chapel. Together with a group, the most popular young men of the city, they have woven and embroidered the gold and yellow peplus, the typical garment worn by Greek women. This will be given to the goddess together with the sacred vases and other offerings. The ceremony includes parades of the city magistrates, priests, members of the city corporations, and the aristocracy, on horseback, like the military leaders. Then come senior citizens waving olive branches, carts, and above all the winners of the games held during the days of celebration that end today with a mass ritual of cleansing, or purification.

The celebrations begin with musical and literary competitions, followed by competitions of sports and gymnastics. Next come the carriage races, the displays of dancers wearing armor and finally the races where the runners carry lighted torches. Today, at the end of the procession, the athletes, musicians, and poets will be awarded with prizes in the heart of the Acropolis and in the presence of the gods and all the people of the city.

The prizes awarded in the races

The winners of the Panathenaic races are awarded laurel wreaths and amphoras, or jars, of oil produced from the sacred olive groves. These are the famous Panathenaic Amphoras, which are decorated with an armed figure of Athena on one side and on the other a decoration symbolizing the discipline in which the athlete triumphed. The winner of the race can win up to 100 amphoras!

WHEN ARE THE THESE CELEBRATIONS HELD?
The minor celebrations are held each year, but the Great Panathenaea Ceremonies in honor of Athena, with their wealth of races and competitions, are held every four years. The festival lasts nine days and begins at the end of July, which is considered the first month of the year in Athens. The Greek name for this month comes from the hecatomb, or mass slaughter of all the animals sacrificed on Athena's altar on this occasion.

THE LOWER TOWN

The Agora

If the Acropolis is the spiritual center of Athens, the Agora, the main square, is the center of a large part of the public life of its citizens. Here the Athenians meet to talk, buy and sell, make deals, settle arguments, form associations, gather information about subjects of general interest or even just see friends, wander around, and waste time.

The Agora in Athens is a vast area in the city center between the potters' quarter and the Acropolis. It is 750 feet long and 550 feet wide. It is surrounded by important public buildings and porticos, or arcades, where you can find shelter from the sun, the rain, or the cold. It is also decorated with monuments, statues, and fountains and shaded by large trees. At the point where the altar of the Twelve Gods stands, you will find the crossroads of all the most important roads in the city. From this point all the official distances from all the other centers of the region are measured. Since the political life of Athens throbs inside its important public buildings, in the square and in the nearby streets, merchants, farmers, shepherds, artisans, fishermen, and potters from all over Attica gather each day to sell their products. The Agora holds the fruit, vegetables, cheese, fish, meat, oil and wine markets,

ONCE UPON A TIME IN THE AGORA!
In ancient times the Agora was used for meetings of the people's assembly. Later, from the end of the 6th century B.C., the meetings were called every nine days on the Pnice Hill. Other public events have gradually moved to more appropriate places, for example, the athletics to the stadium; the theatrical events, the dances, and the poetry competitions to the theater.

together with the markets selling wood, pots, materials, papyri, and books! The goods are displayed on the ground on mats, or more often on carts, under the shelter of a tent, or in huts made of skins. Each stall stands in its assigned place, for which a tax has been paid. The Athenians wander through the market full of curiosity. They bargain, haggle over prices, and cautiously watch ten civil servants employed to make sure that the rules of order and hygiene are fully observed.

The monuments in the Agora

Two huge porticos, or arcades, mark the extremes of the northern part of the square. The first is multicolored and decorated with splendid pictures of historical and mythological subjects. The second is the covered walkway, where once the ruler and chief magistrate, the major authority in the city, used to administrate justice. On the west side we find the principal public buildings of Athens: where the citizens' council meets; the sanctuary of the goddess Cybele, the great mother of the gods, which holds the public records; and finally the circular building, where the meetings and banquets of 50 members of the senate, are held.

The Lower Town

The Council

After wandering a while among the market stalls and maybe quenching your thirst with a nice slice of watermelon, you can visit one of the most important public buildings in the Agora, the Council House. This is the greatest symbol of Athenian democracy. This palace is the seat of the council of the city-state, or *polis*. The council is made up of 500 members elected by drawing lots, 50 for each one of the 10 tribes into which the region of Attica is divided. In this way you will be able to observe one of the many meetings that make the political life of Athens come alive. The sessions are not open to the public, but are held each day except on public holidays.

But what are the responsibilities of the representatives of the people who crowd the steps of this place, sacred to Zeus, to whom the altar at the center of the hall is dedicated? The councilors make important decisions regarding legislative, executive, and judicial matters. Their recommendations are then approved by the General Assembly of the Athenian people. They also monitor the work of the magistrates, assure the application of the decrees issued by the General Assembly, deal with the foreign ambassadors, supervise state spending, and ensure the upkeep of the fleet together with that of the most important public buildings.

The representatives hold office for one year during which they are paid a symbolic salary of 5 oboli per day. This is a rather small amount when you consider that the daily salary of a laborer is about 2 drachmas—more than twice the amount!

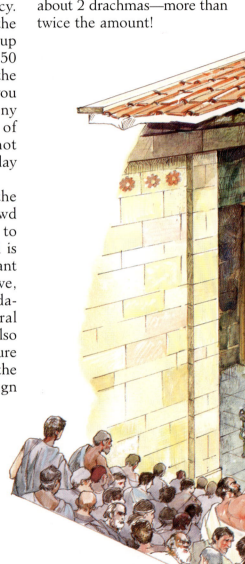

A stone allotment machine used when selecting representatives to public office.

Everyone may have a turn
By law, each male Athenian may not be elected as a council member more than twice in his lifetime. In any case, since there are around 40,000 male citizens, and the council has 500 members, each man who wishes to do so has the opportunity to be elected to take part in this democratic institution at least once. Besides taking part in the council, all citizens, except women, slaves, and foreigners, may personally take part in the General Assembly of the city-state.

WHO ARE THE CANDIDATES?
All the citizens from the 10 Attican tribes who are at least 30 years old may be candidates to become members of the council. After being awarded a seat, before taking office, they have to undergo a tough examination given by the outgoing councilors. If they pass the exam they are sworn into office. During their year in office, they are exempt from military service and have the right to the places of honor at the theater.

Beans and elections
To avoid votes being bought or corruption of any kind, the council members are selected by drawing lots. The Athenians believe this is the way the elections will both respect and carry out the will of the gods. The terracotta tokens bearing the name of each candidate and the dried beans are put into two separate urns used for the election. Half the beans are white, half black. The names are drawn out one by one, together with a bean for each name. If the bean is white, the candidate has been elected.

EDUCATION AND HEALTH

The High School and Gymnasium

I agree, it is not much fun to talk about school while you are in the middle of a trip. However, if you are interested in knowing what the Athenians think about the subject, you can take the road that leads from the Dipylon to the *Akademeia,* or the academy, the wood sacred to the Athenian hero Akademes. Here, in a garden shaded by plane and poplar trees, the Athenians come to stroll and to relax. Here, too, the 12 olive trees sacred to goddess Athena are cultivated. These are the ones that provide the oil awarded as prizes to the winners of the races and competitions during the great festivals of the Athena worshipers. But this place is above all the seat of one of the most famous schools and gymnasiums in Athens, the Akademeia. Plato, one of the most important Greek philosophers, teaches here.

The school and gymnasium is a true cultural center, where the young men improve both mind and body, the two inseparable aspects of the Athenian education, known throughout history as *paideia*. The building is divided into different parts. First there is a long, covered gallery used for training and for running races during the winter. Then you will find an open-air athletics track, a hall with a large pool where the athletes can wash, rub their body with oil, and cover it with sand or dust to protect the skin, or scrape it off with a bronze scraper used for this purpose. There is a gym, an open space surrounded by arcades, onto which the changing rooms, the classrooms and the teachers' lodgings face. In the gym the young Athenian men keep fit, practice sports, and train to fight with the aim of encouraging the healthy and well-balanced development of their bodies. The youths pant and toil under the guidance of a teacher, or gymnastics master, who wears a purple tunic. He observes them and corrects them if necessary, shaking a long, forked stick. They also learn the humanities, music, mathematics, and philosophy. The school and gymnasium is a place where the young men learn the virtues, or *arete,* needed to be future citizens of the polis.

Gymnastics

Between the ages of 12 and 18, after having attended school and learned the arts of music and the humanities, the young Athenian youths are entrusted to the gymnastics master. The pupils are divided into two classes, the youths from 12 to 15 years old, and those between 15 and 18. They practice the exercises in the nude. From a small vase they rub olive oil all over their bodies. They do their exercises to sweet melodies played on the oboe.

The school in Athens

In Athens the state does not require youths to attend school. Teaching is done privately and paid for by the families. The teachers work in their own homes. So, the poorest can only just write, while the more comfortably off are entrusted to a teacher around the age of seven, who trains them to be well-mannered. From the humanities teacher they learn to read, write, and know the texts of Homer. They also tackle arithmetic and music. Guided by an experienced player, the young men also learn how to play the lyre and the oboe.

EDUCATION AND HEALTH

The Asclepieion

The Greek god of medicine is Asclepius, the son of Apollo, who is credited with possessing extraordinary therapeutic, or healing, powers and the magical gift of performing miraculous cures. There is a sanctuary dedicated to him in Athens, the Asclepieion that is found on the southern slopes of the Acropolis.

Here you can find a temple with an altar, an arcade that serves also as a dormitory, where the sick can lie down at night waiting for the god to appear. There is also a sacred spring where the sick can purify themselves and perform the ritual bathing before they experience communicating with or receiving answers from a god. You will also find a sacred well for the consecrations and finally the building that houses the pilgrims.

The best moment to experience the special atmosphere of this sanctuary is in the evening, in the moonlight, when a silver light illuminates the leafy branches of the olive trees and seems to make the silhouettes of the houses flicker. Everyone—the sick, the pilgrims, and the visitors—come to Asclepieion after dusk. They believe that the presence of the god can be specially experienced during a night's sleep. Sleeping for one night in the sanctuary is commonly

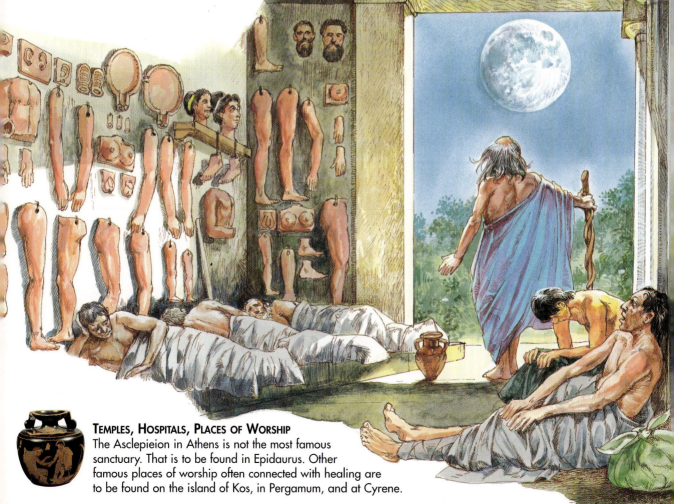

TEMPLES, HOSPITALS, PLACES OF WORSHIP
The Asclepieion in Athens is not the most famous sanctuary. That is to be found in Epidaurus. Other famous places of worship often connected with healing are to be found on the island of Kos, in Pergamum, and at Cyrene.

believed to help the god Asclepius appear in the dreams of the sick. It is also believed to ease suffering and disease. Because of the atmosphere of the place and the effects of self-hypnosis, it seems to lead to recoveries that are like miracles.

Proof that this happens quite often are the numerous offerings hanging on the walls of the arcade. Different parts of the human body—legs, arms, eyes, ears, hands, modeled already in a painful state—are reproduced in small terracotta sculptures. They are offered and dedicated "for grace received" to the god of medicine by those who have benefited from his powers. Some are even dedicated to his wife Salute (Health), or to his priestess Panacea, "she who heals everything."

Miraculous powers!

Asclepius is believed to appear in person in people's dreams or to appear through certain animals that are dear and sacred to him. Believers tell the tale that one of Asclepius' tame snakes appeared in a patient's dream where it was sucking his big toe. When the patient woke, he remembered having dreamed of a noble-looking young man who was medicating his foot. Even the saliva of the dogs that live in the sanctuary is said to have healing powers. It is supposed to heal sores and wounds.

ENTERTAINMENT

The Theater

You will already have had a chance to enjoy the colors and aromas of the Attican spring. In March many people travel to Athens from all over Greece, including businessmen, tourists, even foreign diplomats!

All this activity is because the celebrations the Athenians dedicate to Dionysus, the god of growth and springtime, are about to begin. The festival is called the Great Dionysian Festival. The celebrations last five days and take place in the sanctuary of Dionysus Eleusis (from the name of the village where the worship of Dionysus began). Here, there is a theater dedicated to the god of rapture and excitement. Here you can also see theatrical performances that take the form of competitions. They are organized by wealthy Athenian citizens, whom the state allowed to present the tragic choruses at their own expense.

You will only understand the true value of this extraordinary occasion if you mingle with the people present in the theater. It is both a social and a religious event, where gods, heroes, and mortals each recite their own roles. After a torchlight procession at nightfall, during which the statue of Dionysus is carried to the center of the theater, a priest performs the purifying ritual of sacrificing a piglet on the altar in the orchestra.

WHO IS ON THE STAGE?
The theater of Dionysus is situated on the slopes of the Acropolis. Its huge area holds an audience of up to 17,000. The seats for the priests and magistrates are nearest the stage. The entrances to the stage are at either side of the orchestra, the semicircular space where the chorus moves around Dionysus' altar. Behind is the stage, the scenery, and the actors. Above the stage the flats and scenery are hoisted, together with the equipment used to create the special effects.

Then a herald accompanied by the sound of a trumpet declares the festival open. Comedies and tragedies are performed for four days running! The audience applauds, whistles, fidgets, and generally voices its opinion. When all the works have been performed, the public has to vote to select the best one.

Actors or audience?
In Greek theater, the actors wear special masks to play their roles. The masks represent different types of human beings and also amplify the actors' voices. The female roles are always played by men. The chorus sing and dance in the "orchestra" to the sound of an oboe, at various times in the performance. During the Great Dionysian Festivals the audience see no less than 15 to 17 theatrical works in four days. The performances are interrupted by only short intervals. People bring or buy food and drink and never leave the theater! A ticket costs two oboli, only one-third of a drachma. The poor are paid for by the state from a special fund.

ENTERTAINMENT

Dirty sports

In the stadium, the athletes race in the nude as they do in the gymnasium. People called aleiptes massage them to loosen up their muscles and then smear their bodies with oil. During the games their bodies are soiled with dust and sweat, which can be scraped off with a special scraper. For one event, the area in which the contest takes place is flooded with water on purpose. The opponents fight in the mud, shouting and bleeding.

The Stadium

Outside the city walls, to the southeast of the city, stands the Athens Stadium where the foot races are held. If I were you, I would not miss it! Go on! Find a place up the tiered steps next to the many spectators who follow these events with passion and anticipation.

The stadium has an athletics track, 605 feet long, made of beaten clay. It is surrounded on three sides by stands for the spectators. At the start of the straight stretch, the athletes draw up along the starting line, ready to dash toward the winning post. There are various types of races: the stadium, the double stadium, four stadiums, and the long-distance race of 24 stadiums, about 2.75 miles. Today you are really lucky because you will also be able to watch other kinds of competitions, for example, the long jump, or jumps with weights to balance the movements of the arms. The competitors in this event compete carrying weights made of stone or bronze weighing more than 11 pounds. Other events you will see are throwing the discus or the javelin.

Then there is wrestling, probably the most typical Greek sport. The winner is the person who stays upright after having forced his adversary to the ground. You will see boxing matches, too. The opponents fight with their hands bound with leather strips. One event seems very violent, or not sportsmanlike, but you can judge for yourself.

Ready, set, go!
A clever device helps give the athletes a fair start to their race. They line up inside a triangular space paved with marble, where a series of grooves fan out from a pit in the center where the race judge stands. Ropes are fixed to run along the grooves. The race judge holds the ropes in his hands. They are connected to posts standing beside each competitor. A horizontal bar rests on each post. With just a single tug on the rope the race judge makes the bar drop, thus opening the starting gates. A split second later, the athletes spring forward to try and catch the wind, the prizes, and glory and to adorn themselves with the highly coveted woolen band that the race winners wind around their head, arms, or legs.

Arts and Crafts

The Potter's Workshop

After all the emotion of a visit to the stadium, there is nothing better than to "plunge" into the most picturesque quarter of Athens, where the potters work. It is to be found to the northwest of the city, near the Dipylon. Here you will find the most famous craftsmen and artists in the whole of Greece, working in tiny shops or workshops where workers and apprentices learn the techniques of the trade. They create splendid vases destined to grace the homes and banqueting tables of the Athenian aristocracy and to boost the international trade of the region.

The clay is extracted from the quarries of Amaroussia, then mixed with red ocher, which gives the Attican pottery its characteristic color. Sheets of clay are prepared, ready for use. The potter uses a very simple wheel to shape and create different forms. After having smoothed and rubbed down the pots, he puts them out to dry in the sun. After this

ARTISTS' SIGNATURES
Many famous craftsmen and potters put their signature on their work to increase its commercial value. The potters write the words "made by" next to their name. The painters write "painted by" next to theirs. Others, less famous perhaps but none the less talented, just work!

process, amphoras (jugs for wine and water), trophies, vials, drinking-cups, and jars are ready to be painted and decorated by the best artists in the city.

The decorations are done using special varnishing techniques. They are based on mythological themes, scenes from everyday life, scenes from festivals or religious ceremonies, games or sports competitions. Once decorated the vases are fired in the kilns. During this process they become harder and shinier. Then they are displayed on the shelves in the shop to be admired by the customers!

The potters' finances

With the exception of a few small businesses that employ their own workers, the majority of the craftsmen earn on average around two drachmas per day. A jug costs about 4 drachmas, a drinking cup between 2 and 3 drachmas, a small jar just under one drachma. A dinner service for ten costs around 40 drachmas. So, to be able to earn a living and pay the painters and the assistants, the potters are always on the lookout for wealthy clients!

Arts and Crafts

The Workshop Where Bronzes Are Made

There is no public place in Athens without its own statues, sometimes of gigantic proportions! This is the city's way of honoring a famous public figure, celebrating a military victory, or paying homage to one of the gods worshiped by the people. The most important buildings—the temples and sanctuaries—are decorated with splendid sculptures that tell the ancient stories of gods and heroes and show an admirable role model for each citizen of the city-state.

As you stroll through Athens, you will constantly come across a host of characters made from marble or bronze, brightly colored, that will continue to remind you of model and noble achievements. These statues are made so well they almost seem alive, with their beards and hair ruffled by the wind, quivering skin, rippling muscles, alert eyes, copper-red lips, and mouths with teeth painted silver-gold. Not only do they represent the collective memory of the city, they also are the solemn guardians of the traditional Greek virtues.

The sculptors' workshops, which almost resemble building sites, have developed around the Agora and near the sanctuaries. They are like dark, red-hot caverns, lit by the furnaces for smelting the bronze, crowded with terracotta casts, parts of statues still waiting to be soldered, wooden scaffolding, rough stone tools for smoothing the surface. Here the sculptor Policletus creates, ponders, and writes the *Canons*. That is his manual of rules about art, full of precious technical suggestions about how to make statues.

WHY ARE SOME STATUES MADE OF DIFFERENT MATERIALS?
The huge votive statues in the temples are often so heavy and imposing that the artists have to use several different materials to make them. The body is usually made of wood, which is painted or gilded (covered with draped cloth in various colors). The head, arms and feet, on the other hand, are carved in marble, stone or ivory, or in some other precious material. This is exactly the way the multicolored statue of ivory and gold of Athena Parthenos by the sculptor Phidias is made.

Industrial rubbish and waste

Industrial waste is a common sight for the Athenians who wander around the Agora making pottery, or near the smelting furnaces used by the bronze workers. Fragments of glass, vases, tiles, broken statues, piles of coal and ashes, small pieces of metal, scraps of leather, the remains of bones or iron filings are thrown into the street and then stored on abandoned ground or in neglected courtyards.

Waste is even thrown down old wells or into old water tanks after the workshops have been cleared out. Nor is it rare for foul-smelling and even poisonous smoke to belch out from the workshops. Sometimes sparks from the furnace chimneys cause fires. The work environment is often described by the workers themselves as places of physical and mental brutality. The workshops are filthy, unhealthy places, where the workers sweat, are beaten, breathe toxic fumes, and regularly become ill!

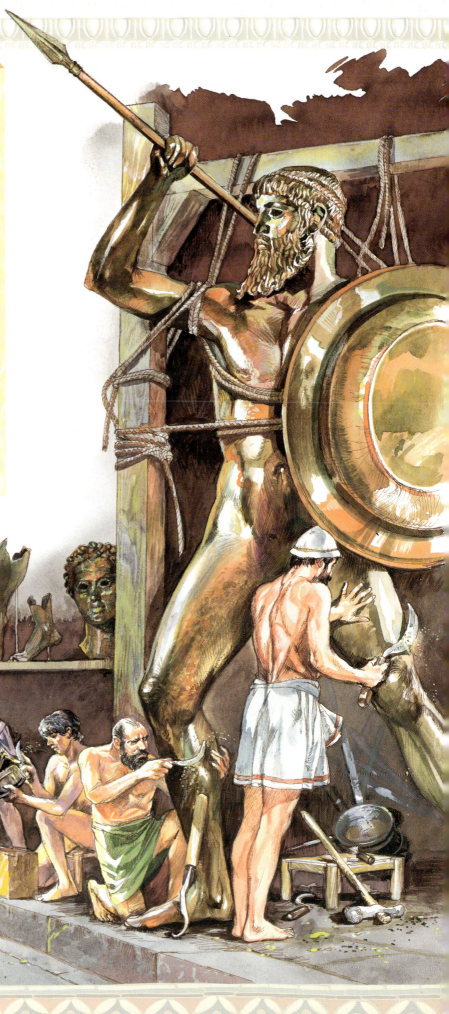

Houses and Customs

The Home

After wandering through the labyrinth of dirty, winding streets, typical of the working class districts of Athens, you will have a clear idea of the miserable lodgings rented out to the poorest families in the city. Now you can go to visit the home of a well-to-do citizen, a famous writer, with whom you had an interesting chat one day while visiting the city. You may be going with the hope of having a free lunch.

Although our host does not seem to be too badly off, nothing about the house would lead you to imagine great wealth. Everything gives the impression of simplicity and modesty. You observe the limited space of the living areas, a few pieces of essential furniture, the absence of luxury and of any kind of decoration. It almost seems that the rich people in Athens make every effort to demonstrate a simple, even frugal lifestyle, inspired by principles of equality and lacking any display of wealth.

The homes of the wealthy Athenians are made and furnished to reflect the principles of the democratic ideals upon which the entire life of the polis, or city-state, is based. Who knows what the slaves or the *metics* (foreigners living in Athens) that you meet in the market might think! The house you are visiting has a two-storied porch on its northern side. In winter this serves as a shelter for the animals, especially their beloved donkey, to protect them from the wind and cold, and in the summer it shades them from the heat. Believe me, few of your host's neighbors could afford such a luxury. He has a well, too! That is a real convenience and saves the young men in the household the chore of having to go back and forth to the public fountain for water. The house has a roof made of red brick and even guttering. The doors are made of a valuable wood, and there is a small *herm* (statue of the god Hermes), a sign of obvious distinction. Once you have entered the hall, an eager door-keeper will let you into the heart of the house. Here is an open courtyard. It is surrounded on one side by storerooms and work rooms for cooking and washing. On the other side you will find the living areas, real apartments built on two stories. On the ground floor you will

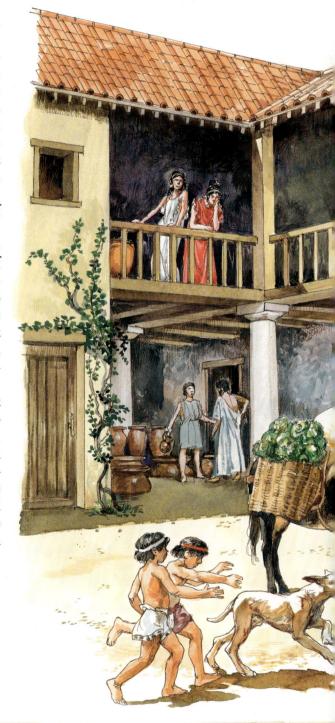

find the banqueting room, together with comfortable rooms where men can meet, relax, and entertain friends. Above this area is the *gynaikeion* (rooms reserved for the women), plus the servants' quarters, which have beaten earth or stone floors, covered with mats or woolen carpets.

Tidiness and cleanliness
The Greek houses are really not models of cleanliness and hygiene. The rich actually do have bathrooms and toilets of the most primitive kind. The more modest homes, often divided between several families, have no space for any form of convenience. Filth and foul smells are constant, in both the kitchens and the communal rooms, where the air is tainted with smoke from the braziers and from the oil lamps and torches. Here the domestic animals find a place to sleep beside the small, hard beds of the humans.

Drafty houses
Greek houses are generally quite modest. The simple, brick walls are made from a mixture of earth and water and dried in the sun. They are rarely plastered. There are a few windows, which have no glass and are closed with wooden shutters. Sometimes the roofs are covered with terracotta or clay tiles, but more often form a terrace where people can sleep outside in the summer.

Houses and Customs

The Symposium

You are right, you did not have much for lunch, but this is normal for your host. However, after an excellent dinner, preparations are beginning for a gathering reserved for the men only. Respectable women and children are excluded, but the men will make an exception for you this time. This special occasion is a *symposium,* an old tradition that helps strengthen the social ties among the Athenian aristocracy. But remember, their refined lifestyle requires them to demonstrate the civil virtues of moderation and dignity even in their excesses.

A group of friends (usually seven) meets in the banquet room. They gather on special occasions or simply to celebrate the arrival of a well-respected guest. They are entertained by young slaves, the *hetairai,* who play, sing, dance, and perform acrobatics. They play games, generally enjoy themselves, and sing hymns in praise of the gods during the libations (see p. 53).

The wine flows, while the guests talk passionately of politics or philosophy. They feast comfortably reclined on *klinai.* They are elegantly dressed, perfumed, and wear wreaths of flowers or vine leaves on their heads. Slaves bustle to serve them. After a toast in honor of Dionysus, they elect the "king of

DIVINE NECTAR
In Greece, wine is by far the most appreciated drink. After a rapid period of fermentation in vats, the wine reaches the Athenians' tables in wineskins made from goat or pigskins, in jars or in terracotta amphoras. It is rarely consumed pure, but instead diluted with water, water and honey, even with salted water or with water flavored with herbs such as thyme, mint, or cinnamon. The ingredients are mixed in large vases. Then, the mixture is poured into jugs or decanters and from these into special cups, which have no base and are shaped like a ram's head, a griffin, or some other mythological animal. The cups are passed around until they are empty.

the symposium." It is his responsibility to decide how to dilute the wine; how many parts of water to use, two parts to three or four to every five. He also decides how many cups each guest has to drink. Whoever disobeys or refuses to accept his orders has to accept a playful punishment, like paying a forfeit, carrying the female oboe player three times around the room! Late into the night, when the series of jokes, funny stories, and riddles has been exhausted, the friends fall fast asleep. Now the slaves have to clean everything up. For them, it is just the start of another day's work.

The game of skill

During the symposium the guests play a game of skill and dexterity in which a target in the center of the room has to be hit with the wine remaining at the bottom of your cup! This must be done from the reclining position on the klinai. Usually the target is a small plate or a vase balancing on some kind of support. The winner receives prizes of fruit, cakes, necklaces, or perhaps even a kiss from a young maiden.

Trips Outside the City

The Necropolis of Dipylon

If you leave the city toward the northwest, just outside the walls you will come across the necropolis, or "city of the dead," of Dipylon. This is the Athenians' cemetery and is named after the double city gate through which you have just passed. Athenian law prohibits burial inside the city, so the cemetery was placed in a quiet, separate area, where the silence and meditation are only broken by the rustling of the leaves and the sound of the wind.

Monuments to the dead line the road. They are vertical stone blocks with sculptures in relief of the dead. So you can admire the figure of a young women with a sweet, melancholy expression, a dove perched on her hand; a man waving sadly to his loved ones before beginning his journey to the Other World; a proud horseman who fell in battle. Some tombs are decorated with the statues of animals: sphinxes, mermaids, bulls, lions, dogs, as symbols of death or as guardians of the dead. You will also notice many tall, narrow marble vases near the graves. These are nuptial or wedding vases that indicate that the person buried there died before he or she was married. Each

Athenian funerals

Athenian law requires its citizens to bury their dead according to their customs. The funeral is an extremely dramatic occasion. After being washed and perfumed, the corpse is wrapped in a sheet and displayed for one or two days on a bed, the face uncovered and the feet facing the door, to allow the soul to leave the room. As a sign of mourning the members of the family wear black, gray, or white. The women cut their hair, scratch their cheeks and express their grief with crying and lamentation. A vase of holy water is placed at the entrance to the house to show there is a dead person inside. Late in the evening or during the night, the funeral procession accompanies the dead person to the cemetery, where they are buried or burnt on a funeral pyre and their ashes placed in an urn. Libations are then offered in their honor, and their house is purified.

monument bears an inscription of the dead person's name together with a brief, familiar description of their trade or profession, their deeds, and their virtues. The largest tombs belong to the members of the wealthy Athenian families. Nearby you will notice several simple stones shaped like cylinders under which lie the remains of the slaves.

Funeral Offerings

Athenian tombs are often decorated with paintings of celebrations or banquets or with the dead person's favorite objects. Sometimes food, wreaths, or even delicate vases are placed on the tombs. The vases hold ointments for the body and are decorated with touching farewell scenes. The intention is to cheer the spirits that dwell in the other world.

Trips Outside the City

The Sanctuary of Delphi

In the region surrounding Athens, you just have to visit Delphi, one of the most important sanctuaries in the whole of Greece. It is situated in a place of unrivaled beauty. Set peacefully on the steep slopes of Mount Parnassus, in a green and scented wood, the sanctuary rises out of natural surroundings where you can almost feel the presence of the gods. In fact, since ancient times, this place has been considered sacred by the shepherds who lived in the area. This was chiefly because of the frequent earth movements, the numerous springs of pure water, the fragrant air, and the disturbing presence of eagles and vultures flying low over the sanctuary.

Delphi is particularly famous for the worship of the god Apollo and for its oracle. The Greeks believe that Zeus, the father of the gods, makes his will known to men through the voice of the priestess of Apollo, the Pythia. Each year, thousands of people come to Delphi from all over Greece to ask for an answer from the gods (an oracle) before making an important decision. After being purified, paying a tax, and sacrificing a goat, they are led to the most secret part of Apollo's temple, the *adyton* (see p. 53). Here the Pythia first bathes herself in water from the nearby Castilia spring. Then she sits on the sacred *tripod,* the famous three-legged stool, amidst the smoke and steam rising from the brazier on which barley flour and laurel leaves have been laid. The laurel tree is the sacred tree of Apollo. In a few moments, you will hear the answer of the gods from the lips of the priestess who has fallen rapidly into a state of mystic ecstasy. Using negative or

MOTIONLESS PRESENCES
Once inside the entrance to the sanctuary, you will notice the silent presence of a large number of bronze statues of famous historical or public figures, heroes or gods. They are votive sculptures that have been commissioned with a tenth of the booty won in war by the different Greek city-states. It is their way of showing their deeply held religious beliefs, their prestige, and their generosity.

positive phrases, or deliberately ambiguous statements, she gives allusive or symbolic answers to concrete questions about health, the need to make a journey, the nature of people's feelings, about guilt, forgiveness, or reconciliation. Would you like to know how well you might do at school this year by any chance?

The navel of the world
At the center of the adyton in the temple of Apollo, you will find a sacred stone. The Greeks believe it has fallen from the sky, and they consider this stone to be the navel, or the center of the earth.

A sacred bank
The prosperous city-states in Greece do not hesitate to celebrate their own power in Delphi by building small temples decorated with splendid marble reliefs called treasures. They were built to house the offerings to Apollo that the sanctuary was no longer able to accept. They guard the riches belonging to each single community. When you walk up the Sacred Way, you can see several, for example, the treasure of Sicyion, Siphnos, Megaris, Syracuse, Cnidus, Thebes, Beoti, Potidaea, Athens, Corinth, and the city of Cyrene. For this reason, Delphi is also like a huge bank.

Trips Outside the City

Attica: The Territory Surrounding Athens

The city of Athens and its surrounding territory are very closely connected. Certainly the capital stands out from the other centers in the region as being more solemn and monumental. But the polis could not grow and prosper without the *kora*, the agricultural region around Athens, where the landowning citizens live and work their estates.

These are grouped for administrative purposes into 140 *demes*. Each *deme* is a kind of commune that is headed by one of the 10 tribes into which Attica is divided. Each tribe sends 50 members to the citizens' council.

The Attican territory is divided into three areas: the Astu, or urban area of Athens; the Paralia, which includes a large area of the coast, unhealthy in places because of the presence of marshes; and the Mesogeia.

The Mesogeia is the most fertile, best cultivated, inland region. The majority of Attica's farms are found here. Oil and wine are produced in abundance, together with fruit, especially figs. These are the main resources of the region, apart from the silver and lead yielded by the mines in Lauro. On the other hand, the farmers do not manage to produce enough wheat and barley to meet the people's needs, so these have to imported from the Middle East and the Euxine, or Black, Sea.

It's great to work in the open air!

The farmers who work in the countryside around Athens have a quite hard life because of the severe climate, the arid, stony land, and the heavy taxes. To plow the land, they use a heavy wooden plow pulled by oxen. They raise sheep and goats for milk, meat for special occasions, wool, and animal hair. Olives are harvested with the aid of long, flexible canes. They are pressed in a mortar or in a primitive stone press. Grapes are harvested by hand and placed in sticky, muddy baskets on the threshing floor. Then, after a few days, the ripe bunches are put into low, wooden basins and trodden for hours under the hot sun to make wine. This is fun, but exhausting! If times are really hard and the harvests poor, the farmers hunt for wild animals or raid birds' nests for eggs.

Water, the fountain of life

The Attica region is quite arid and infertile. Streams and rivers have only a little water and often dry up completely. But, when there is a storm, then they transform into rushing torrents. Water in Greece is as precious as it is rare. This is why rivers, fountains, and springs are considered to be sacred places, inhabited by gods, worshiped above all by nomads and shepherds. It is no coincidence that sanctuaries and important places of worship are usually situated close to these sources of water.

Trips Outside the City

The Port of Piraeus

So, while you are visiting the area around Athens, why not go and take a look at the port of Piraeus? This is the port that serves Athens. Goods and foodstuffs reach here from all over the world, especially wheat and cereals. Trade in these goods is regulated by Athenian state laws. Huge quantities of wheat arrive from Egypt, Sicily, and from the area of the Euxine, or Black, Sea. It serves to feed both the population and the army and, once unloaded, is stocked in enormous warehouses specially equipped for cereal storage.

Among the raw materials to arrive in Piraeus, the supplies of wood from Thrace are of major importance for the dockyards and shipbuilding. In the event of war or invasion, Piraeus can be defended thanks to a series of town walls that protect the built-up area and the docks.

A fortified corridor called the Long Walls ensures a quick trip between the city of Athens and its maritime base. It was built by Themistocles and by Pericles. It is 3.75 miles long and 650 feet wide. This military road contributes enormously to reinforce Athenian supremacy over the sea. The Greeks are excellent sailors.

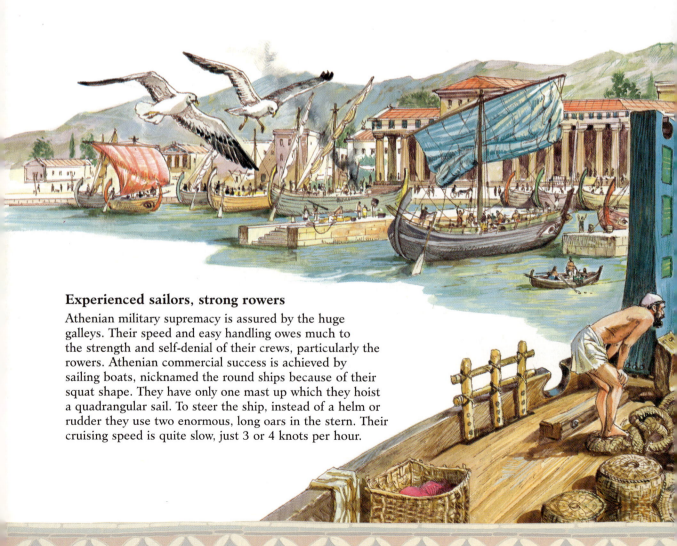

Experienced sailors, strong rowers
Athenian military supremacy is assured by the huge galleys. Their speed and easy handling owes much to the strength and self-denial of their crews, particularly the rowers. Athenian commercial success is achieved by sailing boats, nicknamed the round ships because of their squat shape. They have only one mast up which they hoist a quadrangular sail. To steer the ship, instead of a helm or rudder they use two enormous, long oars in the stern. Their cruising speed is quite slow, just 3 or 4 knots per hour.

The port is always a place of frantic activity. All kinds of ships plow through the dock area waiting for a mooring or ready to set sail. Along the wharves small fishing boats tie up beside large cargo boats, their holds full of goods. In the drydocks, ship repairs and maintenance are carried out. Huge *triremes*, or galleys, are designed and built in the shipyards. Along the wharves, porters unload the ships, while the merchants negotiate, trade, make deals, and pay the Athenian state a customs duty equal to one-fiftieth of the value of the goods.

Armies of merchants!
Piraeus was designed and built by the famous architect Hippodamus of Mileto. Intelligently, he divided the urban areas where people would live from the areas where trade and civil activities would be carried out. The maritime suburb, apart from its temples and public buildings, has three separate ports. To the southeast lie the ports of Zea and Mounichia, with their fortified shipyards. The Athenian naval fleet is based here. To the northeast lies the great port of Kantharos, the center for commercial trade.

The Armed Forces

Athens: War

For Athenian citizens, war is a constant fact of life. Periods of peace are just a brief truce, or rest, before the explosion of another conflict. In order to survive and prosper, the Athenian democracy needs to exercise total control over the trade routes upon which it depends for supplies and keep its unrivaled supremacy over the other Greek city-states.

Thus, a complicated political and military system is at the base of the polis. A network of strategic alliances and diplomatic initiatives, like the Delos-Attican League, work together with the organization of a powerful war machine. An army of foot soldiers collaborates with a military fleet over 300 warships strong. These *triremes*, or warships, are about 165 feet long and 25 feet wide. They are named after their three rows of oars, arranged on three levels. These oars make them fast and capable of making powerful and coordinated attacks. Their prow is equipped with a sharp rostrum, or beak, for ramming enemy ships. It is decorated with two huge painted eyes that serve to frighten the enemy but are also believed to protect the ship from hostile forces and are thus believed to have magic powers.

The triremes are made of pine. Only their keel is reinforced with planks of oak. They have a single sail that is lowered when the ship is engaged in battle. The triremes adopt an efficient battle strategy. After having sailed around the enemy ships, they steer toward them at full speed to sink them. The foot soldiers they carry on board have to be ready to board the enemy ships.

Although the citizens of Athens feel a strong duty to defend their country and are ready at any moment to leave their home and family to serve the network of strategic alliances, they do try to avoid running into a fight. Instead they enjoy the pleasures of bathing in the sea and eating ripe figs.

Glory and honor: It is great to be a soldier!

The armor of well-to-do citizens who make up the infantry corps is made up of a helmet, a bronze and leather cuirass, and a round shield, also made of bronze and leather and decorated with a frightening design. This illustration is also believed to be *apotropaica,* something that is believed to protect or drive an enemy away (see p. 53). Soldiers carry a wooden lance with a metal point and a short, double-edged sword. They are expected to equip themselves at their own expense. They receive a very small daily traveling allowance and have to provide their own food, which they probably buy from the merchants who follow the army. Finally they have to face long marches, fierce fighting, massacres, raids, ruin, disfiguring wounds, and painful misfortunes.

Charge!!!

The infantry of well-to-do citizens is the backbone of the Athenian army and fights in closed formations called phalanges. These move against the enemy chanting a warsong, the paean. *The assault is carried out by a compact row, or rank, of lancers that creates a tremendous attacking force. They have the task of breaking the unity and strength of the enemy lines. Once they have penetrated these, they engage in fierce hand-to-hand fighting until they gain the upper hand with the help of auxiliary troops of archers and stone-throwers, recruited from the poorest inhabitants of Athens. During the attacks or periods of siege, the Athenian army uses catapults, battering rams, and a dreadful mixture of burning coals and sulfur.*

ATHENS TODAY

Present-Day Athens

Athens today is both a historic city and the capital of modern Greece. Generally considered to be the birthplace of western civilization, Athens is a sprawling city of almost four million people. It is home to about one-third of Greece's entire population. Although modern Athens is built in concrete and is said to have the worst smog and traffic of any city in Europe, evidence of its legendary history and splendor can still be found almost everywhere you go in the city.

The Ancient Agora of Athens

The Agora of ancient Athens was an open space where the citizens of the city could meet. Each trade had its own space. Under the Romans, the Agora was a covered market with columns. Some can still be seen. What you see today is the result of a restoration carried out by several American programs and the government of Greece between the 1930s and the 1960s. As you approach the Agora, you will see the Theseum, built in the 5th century B.C., and the best-preserved of the ancient Greek temples.

Delphi

Do not forget to take a trip outside Athens to Delphi. This was where the famous oracle was located. Here the cities and states of the Greek world competed to leave the oracle the most valuable gifts, making Delphi a city of fabulous wealth, too. Visit the Sanctuary of Apollo, where the famous priestess pronounced her prophecies. Walk along the olive-covered hillsides to marvel at the ancient semicircular amphitheater, which is still used for summer festivals. Do not forget to test its amazing acoustics. If you stand in the center of the stone stage and whisper your lines, a friend sitting on the uppermost row of stone seats will still be able to hear you.

Theater of Dionysus

To your left as you climb the southern slope of the Acropolis is the Theater of Dionysus, the oldest of all the world's known theaters. Here were performed the works of the four greatest Greek playwrights—Aeschylus, Aristophanes, Euripides, and Sophocles. Historians estimate that the theater once held as many as 17,000 spectators. Only parts of the stone seats, made in the 4th century B.C. have survived. Today, in the summer, open-air performances of music, theater, and dance take place as part of the Athens Festival in the Herod Atticus Theater, built A.D. 161.

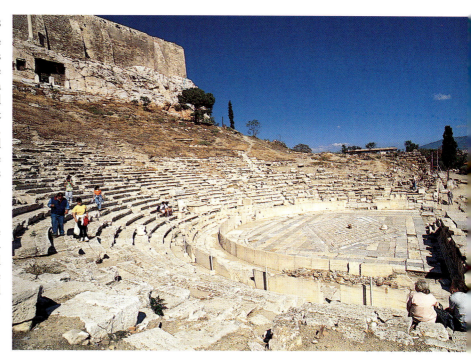

The Panathenian Stadium

The Panathenian Stadium is where the first modern Olympic Games were held in 1896. Since Greece had been the site of the ancient Olympic games, Athens was the natural choice to host the first modern version, too. The reconstruction of the ancient stadium started in 1895, just one year before the games were scheduled to open. An estimated 40,000 spectators attended the opening ceremony. The price for admission was just 16 cents. At these first, modern Olympic Games, only first place and second place finishers were awarded prizes—a silver medal for first, a bronze for second, and crowns of olive branches for both.

ATHENS TODAY

Kerameikos or Potters' Quarter

Kerameikos is a quarter of Athens to the west of Harmony Square. The name means "the potters' quarter." The outer part of the quarter was near the public cemetery. Some of these ancient tombs and burial monuments can still be seen. Today the area has a beautiful Greek Orthodox church, in addition to a Roman Catholic house of worship.

The Acropolis

The Acropolis dominates all views of Athens. After 2,500 years it still inspires wonder. The climb up the rock is steep, but it is well worth the effort. The monuments date from the prehistoric period to the end of antiquity. Do not miss a visit to the Acropolis Museum, which will help you understand the role of the Acropolis as the city's spiritual center. The maidens supporting the south porch of the Erechtheion, a sanctuary, are copies of the famous originals. While four of the six originals are in the Acropolis Museum, the fifth is being restored, and the sixth is in a London museum. It is one of the famous marbles, shipped to Great Britain by Lord Elgin in the early 1800s. Legend has it that the maidens weep for their "abducted" sister, and patriotic Greeks still want the Elgin Marbles returned. Recently, the Greek government has agreed to build a new museum to house the Elgin Marbles. The Greek people remain hopeful that these treasures will be returned in time for the 2004 Olympic Games, which Athens will host.

Piraeus

Located 5 miles (8 kms.) from Athens on the Saronic Gulf, an inlet of the Aegean Sea, Piraeus is the seaport for the Greek capital. As the largest port in Greece, where international shipping is a major part of the economy, Piraeus is home to scores of shipping offices. Piraeus is also the most important manufacturing city in Greece. Many kinds of ships travel on its waters. Small ships carry passengers from Piraeus to the many nearby Aegean islands.

The Parthenon

Constructed and decorated between 447 and 432 B.C. the Parthenon is, without doubt, the crowning glory of Athens and one of the treasures of civilization. The beauty, harmony, and grace of this monument make a lasting impression on all who see it. The columns of the Parthenon were designed to lean slightly toward the center, leaving the impression that they are bending slightly under the weight. None of its vertical lines are absolutely straight. Built of white marble from Penteli, the Parthenon housed the golden-ivory statue of Athena, the work of the famous 5th century B.C. sculptor Phidias. Today, admission to the interior of the Parthenon is prohibited, so that restoration of the site, begun in 1983, can continue. This will not, however, prevent you from admiring the splendor of this work.

Some Important Facts

Archaic and aristocratic Athens • Athens was one of the principal city-states in ancient Greece. In archaic times it was governed by kings, who were later overthrown by the *eupatrids* (see p. 53).

From the 8th century B.C., the aristocracy took over the leadership of the city, and Athens was dominated by the archons, who were rulers and chief magistrates. In 624 B.C., the archon Draco drew up the first code of written laws in the attempt to check the absolute power of the nobles while still protecting their privileges. But the laws were so severe and unfair they caused riots among the population.

From Solon to Cleisthenes • Solon became archon in 594–593 B.C. He introduced many social and political reforms that encouraged the development of the democracy. The citizens of Athens were divided into classes and, depending on their wealth, had access to positions of public office. Solon attempted to limit the growth of large estates and abolished the terrible practice of slavery for debtors. However, the poorer citizens, the smaller farmers, and the craftsmen were dissatisfied with Solon's reforms. For this reason they supported the rise of the tyrant Pisistratus. He promoted agriculture, small property owners, and trade, strengthened the army, and improved the people's living conditions.

It was his son Hippias who proved a true tyrant and who was overthrown by the aristocrats' revolt in 510 B.C. In 508–507 B.C., Cleisthenes became archon and introduced a series of democratic reforms. The majority of public offices became elective. The chosen candidates were elected by majority vote by the citizens who were directly involved in governing the city. This is how the model of the *polis*, or city-state, was born.

Athenian power • During the Persian Wars (490–480 B.C.), Athens revealed itself as a tremendous military power because of the strength of its army. So it became the political leader of the other city-states in the victorious campaign against the Persian kings Darius and Xerxes. It was an extremely tough conflict. Athens paid a very high price in terms of losses and devastation. However, the wars against the Persians served to reinforce the links between the different city-states in Greece, who were always fighting among themselves. This led to the creation of the Delos League in 477 B.C.

The Delos League was a military alliance formed for the purpose of defending Greek territory in the case of Persian invasion. Apart from Athens, its members were the Aegean islands and the cities in the regions of Anatolia and Thrace. Within the league, Athens had control of the common funds, which gave it the opportunity of strengthening its naval fleet and controlling maritime traffic.

Pericles • Head of the democratic party, member of the council of strategists, and one of the most famous magistrates in the city, from 462 B.C., Pericles was the undisputed leader of the extraordinary economic, artistic, and cultural development of Athens. During his period of government the conflicts with Sparta began, which in 431 B.C., exploded into the Peloponnesian War. The clashes ended 27 years later with the defeat of Athens. The city lost its supremacy and for a year was forced to accept the political model of the Spartan regime, rule by the so-called "thirty tyrants."

Hellenism • During the 4th century B.C., Athens began to create democratic institutions again. But the city had started its slow decline. The end of Athenian independence and of its ideals of civilization came with the Battle of Chaeronea, fought against the Macedonians in 338 B.C. They had begun a policy of conquest under the leadership of Philip II, the father of Alexander the Great. Then in 146 B.C., Athens fell under the domination of Rome.

Glossary

adyton (AD-deh-TAHN) the most sacred and secluded area of a temple or place of worship, where the statue of the god is often kept

aleiptes masseurs who oil and massage the athletes' bodies before a race with oils or ointments

apotropaic (AH-peh-troh-PAY-ik) describes something believed to drive away, or exorcise, an evil spell, to defeat an enemy or ill-intentioned person, or protect someone against bad fortune

arete (ah-ret-TAY) the virtues of Athenian citizenship

demos (DAY-mohs) the people; citizens who hold political rights

Eupatrids (YOU-pa-tridz) members of the Athenian aristocracy in the 8th century B.C. who overthrew the old kings to take over the city's government

gynaikeion (gin-eye-KAY-on) rooms reserved for the women, in the houses belonging to the wealthiest Greek citizens; they held looms, cradles, and couches

herm (HERM) small statue of the god Hermes that is placed in a courtyard or at the entrance of a house and believed to stop evil spirits or sickness at the door

hetairai (Heh-TIE-reye) young slaves who entertain the guests during banquets or symposiums by dancing, playing the flute, or performing acrobatics

klinai (KLEEN-eye) a kind of bed found in the banquet room of the wealthier Greeks' houses, where, during a banquet the guests could eat, drink, and enjoy themselves comfortably lying down, or fall asleep after the celebrations had finished

kora (KOH-rah) the countryside around Athens, the region where the agricultural activities of the city were concentrated

libations (lie-BAY-shuns) ritual or sacrificial offerings of wine in honor of the gods or the dead

metics (meh-TICKS) the foreigners who live in Athens: they are chiefly minor tradesmen or work as laborers for various craftsmen

paean (PEA-un) song of war or victory; originally a sacred hymn in honor of the gods

paideia (pie-DAY-uh) learning or education

papyri (puh-PIE-ree) pieces of paper; papyrus

pediment (PED-ih-ment) a low gable, usually in the form of a triangle, used above a door

polis (PAH-lehs) the city-state

stadion (STAD-ee-on) about 600 feet

symposium (sim-POZ-EE-um) informal banquet held by well-to-do Athenian men

temenos (TEE-meh-nos) sacred enclosed area or space within which was built a temple dedicated to a god

tripod (TRY-pod) three-legged stool where the Pythia of the oracle at Delphi sat to deliver her answers from the gods; also a three-legged support for vessels containing water, meat or wine, and in some cases a prize awarded to the winners of sports competitions

Further Reading

Crisp, Peter. *The Parthenon* (Great Buildings Series). Raintree Steck-Vaughn, 1997.

Daly, Kathleen. *Greek and Roman Mythology A to Z: A Young Reader's Companion* (Mythology A to Z Series). Facts on File, 1992.

Honan, Linda, and Kosmer, Ellen. *Spend the Day in Ancient Greece: Projects and Activities that Bring the Past to Life* (Spend the Days Series). John Wiley, 1999.

Kerr, Daisy. *Ancient Greeks* (Worldwise Series). Franklin Watts, 1997.

Kotapish, Dawn. *Daily Life in Ancient and Modern Athens* (Cities Through Time Series). Lerner, 2000.

MacDonald, Fiona. *The Traveler's Guide to Ancient Greece.* Scholastic, 1998.

Millard, Anne, and Peach, S. *The Greeks.* EDC, 1999.

Nardo, Don. *The Parthenon of Ancient Greece* (Building History Series). Lucent Books, 1999.
 ____ . *Ancient Greece.* Lucent Books, 1994.

Stein, R. Conrad. *Athens* (Cities of the World Series). Childrens Press, 1997.

Index

Acropolis, 6–8, 12–13, 26, 50
actors, 27
addresses, 9
adyton, 41
agonothetes, 29
Agora, 7, 8, 10, 18–19, 32, 33, 48
Akademeia, 21
aleiptes, 28
alliances, 46, 52
Amazons, 14
amphoras, 17, 31
animals, 11, 25, 34, 35, 43
Antesterie, festival of, 11
Apollo, 11, 40, 41, 48
apotropaica, 47
archons, 52
arete, 22
aristocrats, 5, 36, 52
armed forces, 46–47
armor, 47
Artemis Brauronius, 12
artists, 30
arts and crafts, 30–33
Asclepieion, 24–25
Asclepius, 24, 25
Astu, 42
Athena, 7, 8, 12–17, 22, 32
athletes, 21, 28
Attica, 7, 42–43

banks, sacred, 41
barley, 10, 42
bathrooms, 35
beans, 21
boats, 44
body language, 9
bronze workshops, 32–33
burial, 6, 38

calcoteca, 12
calendars, 11
Callicrates, 13, 14
Canons, 32
cemeteries, 38, 50
Centaurs, 14
Ceramico, 6–7
Chaeronea, battle of, 52
children, 11, 36

citizenship, 11, 20, 21
"city of the dead," 38
civil rights, 11
cleanliness, 35
Cleisthenes, 52
clocks, 11
clothing, 9
coins, 8
Corpus Hippocratium, 9
Council (Boule), 20–21, 42
crafts, 30–33
customs, 34–37
Cybele, 19

Delos League, 46, 52
Delphi, 40–41, 48
demes, 11, 42
Demeter, 11
democracy, 20, 52
dentists, 9
Dionysian festivals, 10, 11
Dionysus, 26, 36, 49
Dionysus Eleusis, 26
Dipylon, 6, 38–39
distance, measurement of, 10
doctors, 9
Draco, 52

education and health, 22–25
elections, 21, 52
Elgin Marbles, 50
emigration, 5
entertainment, 26–29, 36
Erechtheion, 50
Eretteus, 12, 13
exercises, 23

farming, 5, 42, 43
festivals, 10, 11, 16–17, 26, 50
fights, 28, 29
food, 10
foreigners, 11
fountains, 43
funerals, 38, 39
furnaces, 33

galleys, 44, 45
games, 11, 37
General Assembly, 20

gestures, 9
Giants, 14
gnomon, 11
gods and goddesses, 7, 11, 12, 14, 40
Great Dionysian Festival, 26, 27
gymnasium, 22–23
gynaikeion, 35

Hellenism, 52
Heritonius, 15
herm, 34
Hermes, 34
hetairai, 36
high school, 22–23
Hippis, 52
Hippocrates, 9
Hippodamus of Mileto, 45
holidays, 11
hostels, 8
houses, 8, 34–35

Ictinus, 13, 14
illness, 9, 33
incubation, 24
industrial waste, 33
inns, 8

Kantharos, 45
Kerameikos, 50
kings, 52
klinai, 36, 37
kora, 42

laurel tree, 40
laurel wreaths, 17
Lauro, 42
laws, 52
length, measurement of, 10
libations, 36
liquids, measurement of, 10
lodging, 8
Long Walls, 44
Lower Town, 18–22

markets, 10, 18–19, 48
Marsia, 13
masks, theater, 27

meals, 8, 10
measurement, 10–11
medicine, 9, 24, 25
Mesogeia, 42
metics, 11, 34
military, 44, 46–47, 52
miracles, 25
Mnesicles, 13
money, 8
monuments, 19, 38–39, 48, 50
Mounichia, 45
music, 23

names, 11
navel of the world, 41
navy, 45
necropolis, 6, 38

oculists, 9
olive trees, 7, 22
Olympic Games, 49, 50
oracles, 40–41, 51

paean, 47
paideia, 22
palaces, 20
Panacea, 25
Panathaic Amphoras, 17
Panathenaea, 11, 12, 16–17
Panathenian Stadium, 49
parades
Paralia, 42
Parthenon, 7, 12–15, 51
pediment, 14
Peloponnesian War, 50, 52
Pericles, 13, 44, 50, 52
Persians, 14
Persian Wars, 52
pharmacies, 9
Phidias, 13, 14, 32, 51
Piraeus, 44–45, 51
Pisistratus, 52
Plato, 21
Policletus, 32
polis, 11, 20, 42, 46, 52
politics, 11, 18, 20

Poseidon, 7, 11, 12, 14
potter's workshops, 30–31, 50
public health service, 9
Pythia, 40

races, 16, 17, 28
residential areas, 8, 9
restaurants, 8
rivers, 43
roads, 4–5, 9, 18, 38, 44
round ships, 44
rubbish, 33

sacred banks, 41
sacred stone, 41
Sacred Way, 6, 7, 41
sacrifices, 26, 40
Salute, 25
sanctuaries, 12, 13, 24, 26,
 40–41, 43, 51
school, 22–23
sculptures, 32, 40
sea journeys, 5
seaports, 44–45, 51
ships, 44–46, 51
shopping, 10, 19
slaves, 9, 11, 34, 36, 37, 39, 52
sleeping in sanctuaries, 24–25
social life, 36
soldiers, 47
Solon, 52
Sparta, 52
speaking, 9
spitting, 9
sports, 22, 28
springs, 43
stadio, 10
stadiums, 28–29, 49
statues, 13–15, 32–34, 40
streets, 8, 9
sundials, 11
superstition, 9
symposium, 8, 36–37

taxes, 11
teachers, 23

temenos, 12
temples, 8, 12–15, 24, 40, 41,
 48, 50, 51
Theater of Dionysus, 49
theaters, 26–27, 50
Themistocles, 44
Theseum, 48
Thesmoforie, festival of, 11
time, 11
Titans, 14
toilets, 8, 35
tombs, 38, 39, 50
toys, 11
trade, 44–45, 51
travel, 4–5
treasures, 41
tribes of Attica, 42
tripod, 40
trips outside the city, 38–45
triremes, 45, 46
Trojan Horse, 13

Upper Town, 12–17

vases, 30, 38, 39

walls, city, 7
wars, 46–47, 52
water, 8, 10, 34, 43
water clocks, 11
wealth, 34, 39, 52
weapons, 47
weights and measures, 10
wheat, 10, 42, 44
wine, 36, 37
women, 11, 35, 36, 38
wood, 44
workshops, 30–33

Zea, 45
Zeus, 12, 14, 20, 40, 51